Resilience:
Grow Stronger in a
Time of Crisis

The *Resilience* Series

Resilience:
Grow Stronger in a
Time of Crisis

Linda R. Ferguson, PhD.

CHANGEMAKERS
BOOKS

Winchester, UK
Washington, USA

JOHN HUNT PUBLISHING

First published by Changemakers Books, 2020
Changemakers Books is an imprint of John Hunt Publishing Ltd., No. 3 East Street,
Alresford, Hampshire SO24 9EE, UK
office@jhpbooks.com
www.johnhuntpublishing.com
www.changemakers-books.com

For distributor details and how to order please visit the 'Ordering' section on our website.

Text copyright: Linda R. Ferguson 2020

ISBN: 978 1 78904 697 7
978 1 78904 698 4 (ebook)
Library of Congress Control Number: 2020937317

A CIP catalogue record for this book is available from the British Library.

Design: Stuart Davies

UK: Printed and bound by CPI Group (UK) Ltd, Croydon, CR0 4YY
Printed in North America by CPI GPS partners

We operate a distinctive and ethical publishing philosophy in
all areas of our business, from our global network of authors to
production and worldwide distribution.

Contents

Previous work

Living Your Purpose: The Heart of NLP. (2014) Victoria, B.C.:
Friesen Press.
ISBN 978-1-4602-1455-8 (Hardcover)
ISBN 978-1-4602-1456-5 (Paperback)
ISBN 978-1-4602-1457-2 (eBook)

All things fall and are built again.
W. B. Yeats

Foreword: Resilience in a Time of Crisis

by Tim Ward, Publisher of Changemakers Books

"What can we do to help?"

In a time of crisis—such as the 2020 Covid-19 pandemic—we all have a natural impulse to help our neighbors. John Hunt, founder of John Hunt Publishing, asked this question of our company, and then offered a suggestion. He proposed producing a series of short books written by experts offering practical, emotional, and spiritual skills to help people survive in the midst of a crisis.

To reach people when they need it most, John wanted to accomplish this in forty days. Bear in mind, the normal process of bringing a book from concept to market takes at least eighteen months. As publisher of the JHP imprint Changemakers Books, I volunteered to execute this audacious plan. My imprint publishes books about personal and social transformation, and I already knew many authors with exactly the kinds of expertise we needed. That's how the Resilience series was born.

I was overwhelmed by my authors' responses. Ten of them immediately said yes and agreed to the impossible deadline. The book you hold in your hands is the result of this intensive, collaborative effort. On behalf of John, myself, the authors and production team, our intention for you is that you take to heart the skills and techniques offered to you in these pages. Master them. Make yourself stronger. Share your newfound resilience with those around you. Together, we can not only survive, but learn how to thrive in tough times. By so doing, we can find our way to a better future.

Tim Ward
Publisher, Changemakers Books
May 1, 2020

Chapter 1

More Than You Think

One jump ahead. That's you. You're always seeing one jump ahead. You are not just curious about what comes next, you like to see what's possible before other people do. Whether you're innovating at work or trouble-shooting at home, you've learned to think on your feet and trust your instincts. You know you can stay ahead of the game and other people come to you so they can stay ahead of the game too.

You might have built a family, a business, a life. You're proud of that, proud of every new skill you struggled to master, proud of discovering that you have what you need to lead. It hasn't been easy, but you don't mind hard work. You keep learning so that you can keep getting better. You're always looking for more tools for your toolkit. You love stretch goals, those goals that are just out of reach. You know you'll do the work it takes to get there.

That work includes understanding people better. You know that you can't expect the best from yourself and others unless you know what is possible. How do people make good decisions? How do you know when to trust your instincts and when to step back and think it through? Communication is an endless struggle, a challenge to get other people to understand and get moving. You need credible information about how people work, so you can get yourself and others to work better.

And suddenly, the world around you changed. You can't stay one jump ahead of a crisis. A crisis is a situation where change is happening, and no one knows where it is leading. Things will get back to normal one day, but there is no guarantee that normal will be the same normal we had before. People use lots of different words to describe their feelings but you know that

3

they all come down to one word: fear. The information you have is scary, and the information that no one has is also scary.

You want to believe that you will be one of those people who steps up in a terrible time and sees the way forward. You don't need to be a hero: you just want to keep it all together and keep your people safe. You want to trust your own thoughts and feelings. You hope that somehow you'll be able to dig in and find new strengths to meet new problems.

There are days when it's hard to hold onto this hope, days when the challenges and uncertainty are overwhelming. The business or career you have worked for years to build could fall apart. The family you love is vulnerable. You need a hug, but hugs are now off-limits. All of the struggles you ever had with isolation or anxiety are pressing on you now. The voice in your head asks, "What makes you think you can get through this?"

Here's what makes me think that you are more than that voice in your head, that the strengths you will grow now are more than you think they will be. I have good information about how the mind and brain and body work, and they are an amazing system that has evolved to make us resilient. And I know that social connection is wired into every human brain, and that social connection is an evolutionary super power that has allowed human beings to make progress under terrible circumstances before. You, as a normally functioning human being, are so much more than that voice in your head.

If you'll let me be part of your social network, if you will let my words be the voice in your head, I'll take you on a tour of you that will show you what I see. You'll learn how to connect to the strengths and experiences that will get you through this time. And you'll develop a blueprint that allows you to continue moving toward what you want in your life. It's a lot packed into a few pages.

It's not going to be an easy read. More than thirty years as an educator have shown me two things:1) There is no substitute for experience. You don't learn by reading; you learn by doing; and 2) Struggle is useful. The work you put into the exercises is what allows you to own the skills and information. You know this. You live this. You work hard because it pays off.

The exercises in this book have been designed to help you find a fresh perspective on your own experience. This means that they will ask you to think about the things that are normally just outside your awareness, or to think about your behavior from a new point of view. Both will allow you to explore how your mind/body/brain equipment works, and how you can leverage your social connections so that you benefit and they benefit.

You will definitely need paper or a journal to record your thinking as you read. You might also want to use a voice recorder for some of the exercises. Record yourself reading the exercise, and then use your own voice to guide your reflections. Neither of these is as good as working with a trusted coach to gain insight, but you probably don't have a trusted coach (if you do, share this book with them). Holding yourself accountable for doing the work is the next best thing.

What kind of work will I ask you to do? All of it is the hard work of not just thinking and feeling, but observing your own thinking and feeling. And then, taking one step beyond what is comfortable or automatic to reach for a new insight or to connect to a strength you didn't know you had. This isn't mysterious. There are many experiences you haven't thought about for a long time. Those experiences can be accessed, but you have to trigger the memory of them. When you do, you also trigger the memory of the strengths, capabilities and understanding that were part of those experiences. You have what you need. You just have to find the right way to ask it to show up.

This might feel strange. It should feel strange. If you are never uncomfortable, you are probably not learning. If you never do something new, you never accelerate your learning. It is a strange feeling to become the observer of your own experience as if you were unfamiliar with what is important or what carries meaning. It's also by far the best way to break through your beliefs about what is possible. When we become very aware of the details, we become aware that we can change the details. When we change the details, we build new experiences out of old ones.

The next chapters will show you how to locate and define strengths in ways you might never have considered. You'll think about an emotion as a set of physiological sensations that you can recognize or change deliberately. You'll understand why other people are so important to your ability to know yourself and to connect with the strengths they see in you. You'll find out why stress is both difficult and compelling and how to manage your thoughts to make use of the energy it contains.

This is a book about you. And you are never yourself alone. A crowd of people live in your psyche and in your memory and sometimes in your daily life. The people close to you might be a big part of what drives you to be better and do better. Yet these same people can drive you crazy. They can be the thing that shakes your careful development of mindset and emotional well-being. They can make you see yourself, but they can also make you doubt yourself. You need strategies for influencing others because it is the only way to predict the influence they will have on you.

And finally, when you have gathered new knowledge of your strengths, it is time to face the central problem: how do you set goals when you don't know what the world will be like? Goals are the key to maintaining both your productivity and your sense of well-being. When you set a goal, you prime your body and brain to look for opportunity in the world. This feels better than going with the flow, because your brain doesn't ever go with the flow. If it has no other direction, it spends all its energy keeping you alive by scanning the world for danger. In a crisis, this can quickly lead to overload. There are too many uncertainties and too many certain dangers.

The best certainty is in you. You can inventory the things you know you want to have in your life. Most of what you want are not actually things: they are abilities and relationships and experiences. As you become clear about what you value, you can become more clear about where you have opportunities to set goals. You can begin to live with more intention, and you can be clearer about where the current situation will support you in reaching for new strengths and achievements.

Does it sound easy? Nothing is easy in a crisis. This book is methodical. It is aligned with the experts who study how people manage thoughts, emotions, choices and relationships. It shares exercises that have helped hundreds of people feel more connected to their strengths. But these techniques require willpower. Willpower is a limited resource. As you work through the book, your willpower will grow. Until it does, it's best to set aside time when your head will be as clear as possible. You don't need to read the whole book at a sitting. You need to walk away with value every time you sit down with the book.

I know this is not what you expected in a short book. I know you are a fast reader, used to grabbing the important concepts and moving on. I know you'll be happy if you find just one idea that you can actually use. This book looks small. But it holds more than you think. It's less like a story and more like a map. Use it to journey into and around the most interesting and important territory you will ever study: you.

Chapter 2

Outside Your Awareness

When you hear the word "self," you probably think of the voice in your head that provides a running commentary on your life and choices. Or you might think of your body, with all of its capabilities and all of its failings. But neither of these gives you a good sense of what you are, what you believe, and what you can do. To grow your strength, you need to know more of yourself. That begins with a better understanding of what a human self is and how it works.

What you mean by self has at least three parts that are all connecting and changing all the time. Your self is your mind. Your self is your body. Your self is the brain that is the keystone of both life and identity. Three different systems are integrated in one bigger system and that system is what we mean by "self." We'll add another component in the next chapter, but this is the foundation. You are your mind, your body and your brain as they function as a single, integrated system.

How does knowing this help you find the strength you need to get through a time of crisis? There are three ways:

1. When there is so much uncertainty, you need to build a foundation out of the things you know to be true. Understanding how your own equipment works gives you a better foundation for making choices and making changes.

2. When you think about the working parts of the self, you open up practical ways to recognize who you are and what you are capable of. You can focus on any one component and gain insights or strengths that will make the whole system better.

3. When the voice in your head recognizes that it is only one part of the system (and not even the smartest part in the system), it's easier to connect with the strengths in other parts of the system.

You are one person, one complex system where all parts work together for the good of the whole. That may be hard to believe, but it is only because the part of you that has a feeling about the statement is your mind: it doesn't represent the whole system. As you understand how the three parts interact, you will learn how to notice what you are thinking or feeling without believing it. That allows you to be curious about your limits and your capabilities. If you don't know the whole story, then maybe there is more to you than it seems at this moment.

The Body's Influence

The limits of our body precipitate every human crisis: it's not just that we are mortal; it's that we seldom have the strength, energy and well-being that we think we should have. This is not about being fit: it's about being fit for conditions we never thought would happen to us. We feel it in our core, in our breath, in restless muscles and random aches and pains.

Your body is more than a container for your real self. Your body is the interface through which you gather information about the outside world and respond to that information with behavior. Without your body, it's hard to know anything at all, because knowledge comes from using your sensory equipment to gather the data your brain needs to predict what will keep you alive.

It matters what you pay attention to. And paying attention is as much a physical act as it is a mental one. It starts in your senses: in what you see and what you hear and the physical sensations that you notice throughout your body. The attention you pay with your body becomes a signal to your brain to record information. When you pay attention repeatedly to something, your brain gives that subject more neural real-estate. That's what neuro-plasticity means. Repeated attention changes our brain. We pay attention when our mind pushes our senses to be more alert to the details.

Because your mind and body and brain are one continuous loop, whatever is present in your body as you think about a situation becomes part of that situation in your brain and whatever is present in a situation you are thinking about becomes part of your physiology. Your state is the total experience of your mind, body and brain at a given moment. All emotions are states, but some states are mindsets (like being in the zone) and some are more physical (like being stressed or relaxed).

This sounds complicated, but it's part of your everyday experience. Some situations make you feel stressed. You know you feel stressed because thinking about those situations triggers changes in your muscle tension. You notice the physical changes, and it makes the stress feel real. You don't just think the situation is stressful: you feel it. And, once you do feel it, any other situation you move into also seems stressful. Because your muscles are tense and your focus is narrow, you are ready to encounter danger. You expect it and then you notice signs that your situation is dangerous.

Your body is connected to your mental strengths

Let's transform that negative cycle into something more useful. Read through the next paragraph and then step back into the memory it describes.

Think about a time you were relaxed in an energetic way, a time you were doing an activity that you enjoyed. Go back to a specific memory of a particular time and a particular place where you were doing this thing with relaxed energy. As you go back to that memory, allow it to build so that you notice more and more of what you were seeing and hearing when you were relaxed. Scan through your body from your head to your toes, noticing where you are moving or still, where you notice temperature or energy, where you notice twitching or tingling. Be curious about every aspect of your physical experience when you are relaxed in an energetic way.

Then write down the first word that comes to mind to describe:

1. What kind of picture do you notice when you are energetically relaxed?
2. What kind of sounds do you notice when you are energetically relaxed?
3. What kind of physical sensation is a sign that you are energetically relaxed?

After you write the three words, you will have released that experience. Choosing and writing the words both helps you to remember the state you have just experienced and helps you become the observer of your own experience.

Now repeat the process with a time when you were ready for something, a time you were fully prepared for what you were beginning. Go back to a specific memory of a particular time and a particular place where you were ready to start. As you go back to that memory, allow it to build so that you notice more and more of what you were seeing and hearing when you were ready. Scan through your body from your head to your toes, noticing where you are moving or still, where you notice temperature or energy, where you notice twitching or tingling. Be curious about every aspect of your physical experience when you are ready to start.

Then write down the first word that comes to mind to describe:

1. What kind of picture do you notice when you are ready?

2. What kind of sounds do you notice when you are ready?
3. What kind of physical sensation is a sign that you are ready?

Now compare the two sets of words. They are not the same words, although you used the same process for both the relaxed state and the ready state. What this tells you is that your state (the combination of your mind, body, and brain) shows up in changes in your body. It also suggests that when you deliberately produce those changes in your body, you will change your state.

Think of some aspect of your current situation that you are not ready for, some part of the situation that makes you feel that you have been caught unprepared. As you think about that part of the situation, focus on your body. Concentrate on that physical sensation that was a sign of readiness until you feel your body start to produce that sensation. Change what you are noticing with your ears and your eyes to match those words from your experience of being ready.

You will probably notice an internal struggle. Either your mind has to give up the idea that you are not ready or your body has to surrender its ability to "do" the ready state. It cannot do what it does when it is ready without changing your interpretation of the situation so that you notice that you are more ready than you thought. This is one of the most tangible ways that our bodies can hold strengths so that we can use them in new situations.

Since your state is a combination of mind and body, you can alter your state either by changing your body (physiology and sensation) or by changing your mind. However, the most common way to know that you have changed your mind is that you have connected ideas to things in the world governed by physics (the world you can experience through your senses). For instance, you probably don't experience optimism in a vacuum; you feel it by imagining good things happening or appearing.

If you imagine good things happening or appearing, you will find yourself feeling optimistic. This means that changing your physiology (your body or your perceptions) can change your mind.

Preparing for a positive mindset

There is lots of evidence that our brains work in patterns called neural or cognitive webs which contain all the information from a given moment in time ("what fires together wires together"). Your brain doesn't separate out "important information" from the sensory perceptions that accompany it. It creates connections between all those inputs and stores them as one pattern.

This means that sometimes one sensation will bring a memory into awareness. You have probably heard a song on the radio that immediately took you back to a very specific time and experience. Or perhaps there is a food from your childhood that triggers a wave of experience when you smell it. These associations form naturally (without conscious intention) as part of the way the mind/body/brain system works.

When particular sensations (a sight, sound, smell or feeling) are deliberately introduced during a memory or experience, these sensations can be used to stabilize the memory of that state and make it easier to retrieve when you need it. Let's use an example. Imagine you notice that you are feeling particularly optimistic; you deliberately focus on the socks you are wearing while you are noticing your optimism. The next time you want to feel that optimism, you put on those socks. As you look at those socks and feel them on your feet, you notice other physical signs of optimism.

Now imagine that you have a tricky meeting coming up, a meeting that will test your endurance and your flexibility. You can put on your optimistic socks as you prepare for the meeting. While you feel optimistic, you mentally rehearse several possible paths to a good result. This means not just thinking them through, but imagining what you will see and hear and feel as you navigate through the meeting and interact with different people.

When the meeting starts, you look down at your socks and you are primed to look for the first signs that you can implement one of the strategies you have mentally rehearsed. Your eyes and ears are attuned to the signals you prepared for yourself, so that you find yourself saying the right thing at the right time. Later you might laugh at your lucky socks. The luck was not in your socks. It was in your deliberate ability to associate something real and present with the state of mind that would be most helpful to you.

Mental rehearsal is a powerful way to prepare for real performance. Pianists who mentally rehearse can run through a piece in their minds with such precision that they show the same progress as they would through physical rehearsal. NBA players spend hours in video sessions. They are not just identifying what did happen; they are running mental practice sessions to develop alternatives for the next time.

Using a physical object to trigger a state makes it easier to manage the mental complexity of preparing for conversations. After you condition a specific, useful response to that object, you can imagine the things that often throw you off, and use the object to rehearse meeting those challenges in a more useful way.

There is strength in movement

You know that movement helps you build physical strength. But you might not have thought about how it helps you grow other kinds of strength. Some athletes are also amazing people with deep resilience and intelligence, but not all. Beyond building health to minimize the impact of stress, it doesn't seem obvious that moving your body could help you move your mind differently.

Unless, you are a mathematician. If you are, you probably know that one proven strategy for solving difficult problems is this: work very hard at the problem; take a walk; let a new approach come to you in an Aha! moment. We think of artists as creative and problem solvers as analytical, but the ability to change frames of reference to discover unseen connections is common to both. And that process is often facilitated by a long walk.

This might not be a time when a long walk is possible. Depending on where and when you read this, you might be confined to a small interior space. Knowing that movement is related to creative thinking might seem as useless in your current experience as knowing how to swim. But it's worth wondering: do other kinds of movement also encourage the brain to put ideas together in new ways?

The short answer is that you can be sure than any amount of time without significant movement is bad for your body, which becomes bad for all of you. So, movement is good if only because it does keep your body functioning. Since you need to find a way to move, why not experiment?

Pick a kind of exercise you like. It doesn't matter if you are on a treadmill or a yoga mat, as long as you are moving in a way you enjoy. Before you start, think about a specific situation or issue that has you feeling stuck. Take a moment and focus. Notice how you see and how you hear as you are focused on being stuck. Notice the places where tension shows up in your body and makes it hard to move. Then give your body a shake and remind yourself that you are not really stuck. You're really ready to move. And just do your workout.

After you finish, take another moment and return to the spot where you were focused on being stuck. Think about that issue again and be curious about what is different now. Notice what is different in your body, and in what you see, and in what you hear. How does this difference open up the possibility of some movement in the stuck situation?

Did you know that small repeated movements are the best way to get out of quicksand? I had often heard the metaphor so I checked with National Geographic. It's true. It takes tremendous force to pull someone out of quicksand, but they can free themselves by wriggling their legs over and over again. We all know that tremendous strength is a kind of super-power. But repeated small movements can sometimes accomplish more.

Know Your Own Brain

Now let's consider your brain. You are carrying around a super-computer that continually seeks to gather information into meaningful patterns that it can use to predict the future. The amount of information your brain can process in a moment is literally mind-boggling. This means that you cannot consciously process the amount of information that your whole system handles easily.

Your brain never does just one thing at a time. It effortlessly manages all your body systems, allowing you to sit up and talk at the same time. It notices what is happening around you and uses that to predict what will happen next and, at almost exactly the same time, it prompts you to take action when it recognizes either danger or opportunity. Your mind will never be as fast, as accurate or as consistent as your brain.

How can you ever discover anything about a processor that is hidden from your conscious mind? We never know exactly what our brains are doing. We can learn from science and approach the subject objectively. We know things about the human brain because science explores them systematically. This is useful in grounding us in what is observable and replicable. We don't have to trust the voice in our heads: we can trust information that has been verified by people we respect. If you have time, read good writers who explain the science. There's a reading list at the end of this book that will give you a great start. If the books seem intimidating, you can always search for TED talks by the authors.

Here's a very quick tour of what the science will tell you. Your brain is exponentially more complex than any computer we have invented so far. It works through electricity and chemistry to process and record vast amounts of information and uses that information to manipulate your perception, emotion, and behavior. It makes most of your decisions before you become consciously aware of making decisions, and it runs most of your behaviors. It has extraordinary, complicated processes for managing time, memory and sensory data.

You can't have a conversation with your brain. Even if you could, it wouldn't go well. Your brain would just keep saying, "You just don't get it." Because there is no way for your finite mind to understand the brain. That's why, for as long as human beings have been telling stories, we have told stories of beings who are way more powerful than we are. On some level, all the stories of gods and superheroes and magical creatures are stories about what a human mind experiences knowing it is tied to a brain that outperforms it in almost every way.

These stories also tell us what human beings have learned about how to work with those superpowers to get what they want. For years, we talked about a mysterious unconscious mind that stored our experience and made choices we could not consciously understand. It makes more sense now to talk about our brain: a component of a human being that has functions but no personality. It's not trying to help you or to hurt you: it's working to do the function it has evolved to do. That seems to be two things: 1) stay alive and 2) seek opportunities for you to get what you want. If you don't want anything, your brain operates in its default mode: scanning the world for anything that could hurt you. It works as if anything that it cannot predict is necessarily dangerous. That means it sends you warm fuzzy feelings about anything that confirms what you already know, and danger signals when you encounter anything new. It's an efficient way to keep you alive: what you can see coming, you can often escape.

Your brain also seems to be remarkably responsive to your attention. Whatever you give your attention to is processed by your brain as a request for more of the same. If you pay attention to what scares you, you get better at noticing what scares you. If you are fascinated by fish, you'll notice fish everywhere. And if you decide that you want something, your brain seems to be able to process incoming data so that you begin to notice opportunities to get what you want.

What's your brain been doing lately? If you're like most people in a crisis, your brain is working overtime to try to predict what comes next. You are probably scared and so your brain is looking for evidence that the world is scary. Because that's what it is searching for, that is what it finds. And, so, you notice ever more evidence that you are doomed. Unless you exert some willpower to change the loops your mind and brain are feeding.

Limit the damage your attention is doing

I understand that the prudent, responsible voice in your head is encouraging your brain to scan for all possible dangers and your brilliantly efficient brain is sending messages into your body to notice all evidence that you are surrounded by danger. But we've already learned that dramatic responses are not always the best way to handle danger. A narrow focus and an understanding of the physical characteristics of the problem you have at this moment can limit the scope of your attention.

Try it now. Instead of thinking about all of the problems and all of the possible problems, just pick one thing you want to solve in the next day or two. Start describing just that problem to yourself. You can do it in writing if you like to write, or you can talk it through if you have space to do that, or you can just sit quietly and reflect. Be as specific as possible in describing what is physically real and present in the situation (just the facts, no speculation about what those facts mean). If you have a feeling about the information, describe it clinically, as a set of physical sensations. If paying attention to your body in this way is new, begin with noticing your head and face and describe anything you feel as you sit with your description of the problem.

Have you tried it? There's a kind of trick to this. As you focus rigorously on what you see and what you hear and what you feel, you will almost inevitably relax. This kind of focus on what is actually coming in through your sensory equipment takes up all your attention, leaving nothing left for the future and its moving terrors. Whether you are doing yoga or mindfulness or hypnosis, when you focus on the present in all its sensory detail, your body gets quiet and your mind gets clear. Even if what you are focused on is the exact limits of the problem in front of you. You don't clear your head by stopping your thoughts. You clear it by directing your thoughts into specific physical sensations.

The magic of asking "what if"

It's hard to think about wanting anything specific when the world is upside down and your brain is telling you that more bad things are about to happen. This is the kind of situation that makes goals seems like daydreams. The only thing that seems worth holding onto has already been lost and the only thing you really want is to get it back. This isn't reality: it's your brain trying to immobilize you so that you don't do anything dangerous. It makes sense to an organism that predicts the future based on the past.

The only way to get moving is to create the illusion that the thing you want has already happened. No one is very sure how the brain knows the difference between what it imagines and what it remembers. If you can imagine something, you can come to believe that your memory of imagining it is the same as remembering that it actually happened. This makes it easier to recreate what you have imagined in real life.

Both imagination and memory have evolved to help us survive and thrive in the present. They have evolved to give us what we need to learn and adapt. When we ask the right questions, our brains throw out clues to what is possible and desirable. One way to try this is to ask yourself "If I woke up tomorrow and the crisis had passed while I was sleeping, what would I notice that would tell me things had changed?"

Try this now. Imagine waking up. The world changed, but you were asleep. It doesn't seem so impossible. You probably feel that happened in the winter of 2020; while your attention was somewhere else, everything changed. So use that to imagine that everything is better, but you didn't see the change happen.

What would you pay attention to and what behaviors would you do if you woke up without the problem that has been taking up all of your attention? How would you get out of bed and start your day? What would be the first sign that things were different? How would you relate differently to other people? What changes in your body when you realize that things are different?

At some point, you'll have an "aha" moment when you realize that something you thought was only possible after the crisis might be possible today. There are things you want to do and things you want to feel, and getting clear on what they are allows you to look for alternatives that are possible here and now.

The power of deliberate repetition

Your brain is the source of all your habits, good and bad. It creates the habits of thought that circle your mind, the habits of perception that have you noticing the same things over and over, the habits of communication that drive you to say, "I'm good" when people ask, and the habits of behavior that mean most of what you do happens before you think about doing anything.

Your mind is a small, weak processor by comparison. It determines only a few things about how you live your life, and it works best on small, finite details. It often tries the same things over and over again, in what seems like a futile struggle to get a different result. The truth is more complicated. Anything done over and over again with conscious attention forms neural networks that can be used again. You would probably call it learning.

Attention intervenes in existing patterns and opens up the possibility of new behaviors. It's just one small point, but it is a leverage point. When you face a big problem, you are probably hoping for a big solution. You are unlikely to get one. The most complex pattern recognition happens in the brain, not the mind. This means that if you were going to find a big idea to conquer your problem, you would probably have done it already. Big ideas are not a strong suit for your conscious mind.

Repetition isn't a strong suit either, but that turns out to be an advantage. We're bad at doing the same thing twice with conscious attention, much less doing it over and over until it becomes automatic. We always make tiny variations in what we do, and our brains automatically collect data on what kind of results we get from those variations. Sometimes we do this with deliberate, conscious attention. While we are not great thinkers consciously, we are determined to get better. And that fierce attention to what we are doing eventually produces both learning and better solutions.

The question is not whether you should do something repeatedly until you get a better result. The question is "where is there something that you can adjust over and over again until you get something you want?" Because when you combine conscious attention with deliberate practice, learning is inevitable. And when learning is happening, other changes become possible too.

Three Things to Remember

1. Your brain and body are always communicating. Listen to your body.
2. Mental rehearsal includes sensory awareness and repetition.
3. Focus attention on what you want, not what you don't want.

Chapter 3

Your Social Self

The mind, the body, and the brain form a three-part self. We all understand that because we are aware of our thoughts and we live in our bodies. We don't see our brains, but we can see them in other bodies and accept that they are a key to staying alive. This three-part system seems complete: it seems to be everything we need to understand a single human being. For most of us, the word "self" means "who we are when we are by ourselves." It means alone.

But we don't live alone. Our super power is cooperation. While you probably don't feel that way in most of your day-to-day life, our reason and our language and even our ability to walk with our heads up all support our ability to do things together that we could not do individually. This is not a matter of personality or individual preference. Whether or not you are a people person, you are socially wired. Your brain is wired for social connection and it engages in social loops in the same way it engages in communication loops with your body and mind.

This means that you can't understand yourself, or manage your mindset, until you also understand that there are other people in your head. Some of them are real and present: they are the people who interact with you. Some of them are real but not present. These are the people you remember from personal experience, whether your memories are days old or decades old. Some of them are memories of people you have paid attention to: these may be public figures, celebrities, the principal at your elementary school or the characters from books and movies. You have wired these people into your brain because they represent information you need to predict and navigate your current and future social connections.

When you are by yourself, you are with a crowd of people who influence your predictions about what comes next. This crowd of people also serves another purpose: they help you recognize parts of yourself that are outside your awareness. You might know your own mind, but you do not know and cannot know your own unconscious processes. Those processes are run by your brain: a processor that is exponentially more complex and more powerful than your mind. Even if you were somehow presented with all the information in your brain, your mind wouldn't be able to process it in the way that your brain processes it. The unconscious mind is not unconscious: your brain processes vast amounts of information whether you are awake or asleep. It is called the unconscious because your mind cannot see it or understand it. It works outside your conscious awareness. You can never know this part of yourself, but you can catch glimpses of it that help you work with it more effectively.

Other people are essential to us in part because they fill in some of the gaps in our knowledge of ourselves.

Think back to a time when you had a conversation where you learned something about yourself by talking to someone else. You might have been talking to someone close to you, or you might have been talking to someone who is very different than you are, someone who has different experiences and assumptions. As you talked, the other person responded to changes in your expression. But you didn't even realize your expression had changed. You can't see your own face, and you are often deaf to changes in your voice.

Your mind is busy with words and ideas and information. It doesn't have the bandwidth to also track your expression. That's why you have had at least one discussion that included the phrase "I am not raising my voice." It's usually said loudly by someone who is convinced that because their ideas are rational, their tone must be reasonable. In the same way, there were times when you had to backtrack to explain something because what made perfect sense to you was not clear to the other person. You discovered that you were working with different assumptions, which means that you had wired this situation into your past experience in a way that is efficient for you but not clear to someone who doesn't share the same past. We only notice our assumptions when someone else notices them.

We sometimes say that someone "knows you better than you know yourself." It might be more accurate to say that person "notices you better than you notice yourself." Because another person pays attention to different cues and attaches them to different assumptions and experiences, they see things in you that you do not see in yourself. And when they communicate that, you have a chance to see yourself through their eyes. You learn something about who you are and how you process and communicate every time you adjust to meet someone else halfway in a conversation. It's not just that we need someone to check our blind spots. It's that the biggest blind spot in your field of vision is the one that contains you.

In a world without mirrors, you could simply stop trying to put on your makeup or shave. But in a world where you have dramatically less access to other people, you lose mirrors for your attention, your assumptions, and your emotions. This is part of the reason that so many people in isolation struggle to regulate their goals, emotions and motivations. When we lose access to the responsiveness and difference of other people, we lose an important channel of information about who we are, how we think and what we want.

You might be struggling to apply this to yourself. That's fair because most of these loops between our social self and our brain and body occur outside of our thinking minds. We respond without knowing we are responding in the same way that people who are paying attention to one another mirror each other's non-verbal behaviors without knowing they are doing it. You'll even notice it in online meetings: if you have video of everyone, you can see people pay attention because they will pick up gestures and postures from one another. You will not often notice it when you are the one mirroring, but you will be able to see it in other people.

The same thing is true with understanding the other parts of the social self. It's easier to see in someone else. You notice it when your sibling suddenly sounds just like one of your parents, or your co-worker says something you heard an influencer say a few hours or days before.

How the Social Self Shows Up

If you could work with a coach, they would sit patiently and wait while you sorted out your responses to these questions. Because you are a socially wired human being, you would be aware of their expectation that you reflect on each, and you would be more likely to pull good answers out of your experience than you are when working alone.

So how can you do your best thinking on your own? First, notice that you are not entirely on your own. As you have been reading, you have been forming an image of me. I am not as real as a coach, but your awareness of my voice as it comes from the page is part of your social network. Next, set a timer and keep your fingers moving (at a keyboard or holding a pen) for the full time indicated. If you're not finished, keep writing. The timer is to help you settle into thinking, not to limit your responses.

1. Think of someone close to you — a partner, family member or long-time friend. As you think about that person, reflect on whether they sometimes remind you of someone else (one of their family members or co-workers, for instance). You might think about how your sibling reminds you of a parent or grandparent, or of how your boss is like their boss. Write for 60 seconds.
2. Give examples of the strengths or behaviors that make

you associate the person you are close to with the other person. Write about situations where you have noticed the similarity or where the same strengths were apparent. Write for 2 minutes.

3. If the person close to you heard this conversation, would they believe they have these qualities? Would they agree that those qualities came from someone else close to them? Write for 90 seconds.

4. Now take a moment to reflect: which of the strengths or behaviors you described in what you wrote are also part of your personality or capabilities? Write for 90 seconds.

Notice that other people reflect your strengths

We are used to talking about exchanges of information and exchanges of emotion. What you might be less used to thinking about is all the things we exchange that are not information or emotion. We don't just communicate data or feelings; we share contagious states. Think of the state you are in as the thoughts, feelings and emotions you use to prioritize information as it comes in through your senses. If you are feeling focused, you prioritize the narrow bandwidth that represents the thing you are focused on understanding or doing. If you are reflecting, you allow more information to come into and out of your awareness. If you're happy, you notice good things and if you're scared, you notice only threats. Some of this filtering of perception is actually physical: under stress, your body changes. This includes your senses: they work differently under the influence of adrenalin and other stress hormones.

One way that your brain and body work together to respond to threats or opportunities is that they match your state to the best outcome in your situation. That's why stress hormones function the way they do. You can also deliberately practice states that you know will be useful to you. If you are an athlete, you might go into a high performance "zone." If you're in sales, you know how to prepare before a meeting and how to recognize signals in yourself that it is time to close a deal. If you're a leader of people, you know that the state you choose to hold is likely to show up in the people you influence.

When you are with other people, they notice your state as it appears in your words, expressions and non-verbal behaviors. As they notice, they reflect back what they notice so you have a chance to witness it in them. Sometimes this shows up as mirroring and sometimes it shows up in expectations. They expect you to be brave or organized or funny and in order to maintain the connection, you find what you need to meet those expectations. Imagine a sudden awkward silence in a meeting. All eyes turn to you to say something, and so you find something to say.

People like it when we meet their expectations because it means that their brains are good at predicting what to expect. This happens below the level of awareness, where our brains apply past experience to make predictions about where there will be either threat or opportunity. It shows up in our minds as that satisfying feeling of being right, even if the original expectation was negative. When we like the connection, we engage in it longer. And that triggers our brains to connect more, both so we can learn from the connection and so that we can predict the outcome of the other person's attention.

You can't know what your brain is processing directly. You can recognize changes in your body that signal a change in state. These changes are fast. You can experience many states in just a few minutes, as you adjust to new information. But your mind won't be fast enough to recognize most of these changes. It works more slowly than your brain and body, and so it will stabilize the states that seem most important, often by labeling them. This is why your self-talk probably includes things like "I have to keep my cool" or "This feels really good." It's a way of reminding yourself to hold onto a useful state.

In the next exercise, you'll have a chance to use the memory of an interaction with someone else to explore how you are able to access and stabilize different states either because the other person evokes them in you or because noticing them in the other person also gives you a template for building them in yourself. In both cases, your social self is active in using the connection to produce the outcome that keeps you safe and moves you toward your goals.

Six Questions for Seeing What You Might Be Missing Now

We know we are well-dressed when people respond to us as if we are well-dressed. We know we are leaders when people wait for us to speak or imitate our behaviors. And we know we can get through a crisis when other people respond to us as the person who can definitely get through a crisis. On the one hand, other people are the mirrors who show us parts of ourselves we cannot see directly. On the other hand, other people's expectations allow us to draw out resources that are part of our unconscious processes.

You've seen the social loops in someone else. Now it is time to look inward and see the influence that a relationship has on you. Because every relationship is about interaction, this exercise asks you to think about two things: 1) what do you feel or experience with another person that becomes an asset in managing your mindset? 2) what do you bring out in the other person that allows you to see a strength that might be outside your awareness or that you might not be confident you have?

It would be best if you had someone you trusted to read the questions and wait patiently while you wrote the answers, without wanting to know what you were writing. Since that might be hard for you to arrange, do the best you can to create an external expectation that you will take the time to reflect on each question. I've recommended minimum time requirements for each, but please write as much as you want (or speak your answers into a recorder).

1. Think of someone important to you who you cannot see physically at this time. Where and when were you with this person? Build up an awareness of what you were seeing, hearing and experiencing in that moment.
2. What's one thing that you feel when you are with this person? (90 seconds)
3. Why is it important to feel that thing? (90 seconds)
4. Why else is it important to feel that thing? (90 seconds)
5. What one thing do you bring out in this other person? (2 minutes)
6. Why is this one thing important to you? (2 minutes)

Now take 5 minutes and write whatever comes to mind about how your interactions with this person help you discover strengths, knowledge or characteristics that were outside your awareness. Include situations where you know the strengths you identified will help you move forward better.

Access Your Social Self without Physical Presence

What happens when there are no other people? Our language is often more exact than it seems. After someone leaves our life, we say, "it feels like losing a part of myself." The truth might be that when we lose a connection, we may also lose access to the part of us that person perceived or expected.

While some of the social self can reach out through remote communication like writing or video chats, much of it feels lost. The truth of the brain/body loops is that they are far more sophisticated and more finely calibrated than anything we can notice or explain consciously. Our imaginations are weak: we often imagine the future and leave out most of the details. The good stuff, the unexpected stuff, is in those details. So, imagining having people with you is often a lot like hanging out with them on a video chat: you have all the basics, but you don't access that part of yourself that you can only know through relationship.

Imagination is relatively weak, but memory is strong. Anything that makes an emotional impact is recorded in detail: not just the important stuff, but all of it. You remember smells and songs and movements and the quality of light in the room when someone special said or did something important. It all gets recorded. That's why the people with the best imagination pay sharp attention to lived experience. They know those experiences will become the building blocks for the future they want to imagine.

The same principle applies when you are alone and you need to access some part of your social self. Your memories of other people contain perspectives and personalities, and they can offer you new ideas about yourself and a problem that you would like to solve.

Here's an exercise that will allow you to experience how this works.

Remember Your Social Self

Read through the exercise quickly, without attempting to imagine anything. You don't need to plan who you want to imagine, but you do need to plan how you will carry out the exercise. If you can, you will find that actually moving around four different chairs adds a powerful layer to the exercise. When your body shows up for an experience, your brain knows you are fully engaged.

For some of you, that won't work. If you have a trusted person with you, they could read you the exercise as you sit and reflect. If not, you could record yourself reading the exercise, or simply pause after reading each section to fully engage in remembering your connections.

Imagine you are sitting in a circle of four chairs. You are sitting in one chair, with the other three around you. Notice what kind of chairs you have chosen, and how it feels to be sitting in your chair.

As we begin, focus on a specific challenge or problem that you would like to move past. Take a few moments and imagine all the components of this situation. Notice what you are thinking, what you are feeling, what you are seeing, what you are hearing and all the physical sensations that are part of your experience as you think about this challenge or problem. Write one word that represents this challenge or problem.

Now look at the chair on your left. In that chair is someone who taught you something, a teacher, coach or mentor. As you look this person in the eyes, allow your awareness to move out of your own chair and into this other person's chair. You are now seeing as they see, hearing as they hear, and noticing what they notice as they watch you approach your challenge. As they watch, they remember times you spent together and qualities they liked or admired in you. When you notice just one thing that they see in you, write one word to capture that quality.

Take a deep breath, and return to your own experience. Sit in your own chair.

Now look at the chair across the circle from you. In that chair is someone who has challenged you or competed with you, someone who made you better but not more comfortable. As you look this person in the eyes, allow your awareness to move out of your own chair and into this other person's chair. You are now seeing as they see, hearing as they hear, and noticing what they notice as they watch you approach your challenge. As they watch, they remember your interaction and notice the strength they noticed in you then. When you notice just one strength that they see in you, write one word to capture that quality.

Take a deep breath, and return to your own experience. Sit in your own chair.

Now look at the chair on your right. In that chair is someone who has loved you. They may be part of your life now or they may be part of your past. As you look this person in the eyes, allow your awareness to move out of your own chair and into this other person's chair. You are now seeing as they see, hearing as they hear, and noticing what they notice as they watch you approach your challenge. As they watch, they remember some of what they loved about you. When you notice just one strength that they see in you, write one word to capture that quality.

Take a deep breath, and return to your own experience. Sit in your own chair.

Now look at the four words you have written. The first word represented a challenge or problem. Look at the next word, the word for the strength noticed by the person who taught you. As you reflect on that word, notice how your perception of the problem shifts. Look at the third word, the word for the strength noticed by the person who challenged you. As you reflect on that word, notice how your perception of the problem shifts. Look at the fourth word, the word for the strength noticed by the person who loves you. As you reflect on that word, notice how your perception of the problem shifts.

Now write one sentence. Say, "Now that I realize I have (strength 1, strength 2, strength 3), here is the next step I can take to solve (word for problem or challenge)."

How Will You Reflect Strength for Someone Else?

You are not just the center of all the mirrors: you are the mirror that shows other people something they cannot see clearly in themselves. When you write or call or video chat with others, you have an opportunity to trigger memories that will help them connect to the strengths and resources held in their social selves.

As we wrap up this chapter, it's time to see what you want to change in the world around you.

Think of someone you know who has a strength or capability that they don't see in themselves or doubt in themselves. Pick a specific situation in which you have seen that strength or capability in them. Write that person's first name.

Now think about that strength or capability. How does it show up in you? How can you hold it in your thoughts and state as you connect with this person? Write one word for this strength or capability.

How will you connect? In this time of social or physical distance, you might not be able to be in the same room. Imagine the difference between sending an email, making a phone call, or showing up for a video chat. As you imagine the best way to connect, also imagine how you will show up in this connection so that it is easier for the other person to access that strength or capability. Pick a time and a channel for connecting.

Now write your commitment to show up and bring out this strength in this person, not by telling or asking, but by expecting and embodying.

"I am going to connect [person's name] to this strength or capability [name it] by making this connection with them [write the time and channel for connecting]."

Three Things to Remember

1. Other people see parts of you that you cannot see yourself.
2. You can grow strengths by seeing yourself through the eyes of other people.
3. You can grow strengths in others by reflecting strengths they have but cannot see in themselves.

Chapter 4

Make Stress Work for You

You might think of stress as something to avoid. You might think of stress as something to seek, a sign that you are doing something difficult and worthwhile. In both instances, we talk as if stress were a thing, like an apple, and that all stress was the same thing. Psychologists have different names for good stress and bad stress, but those terms are not widely used outside academics. We all think we know what stress is.

We also think we know whether or not stress is a choice. This knowledge is based on a combination of what we want, how we think we function best, and how we think other people should function. So sometimes stress is a choice that high performers make because it drives them to excel. And sometimes stress is an effect of a situation that exerts unpredictable and uncontrollable pressures on our ability to make choices and take action. Even then, we look at signs of stress in some people and think, "He's got to get a grip" or "She needs to get that under control."

Those attitudes don't change as quickly as the world changes. But once we are under constant, unremitting stress from conditions that are outside our control, we have an opportunity to think about what stress is doing in our thoughts and our bodies and how to use the energy in stress to drive productive responses instead of driving us (and the people around us) crazy. This is the approach you have used whenever stress has worked for you, whenever you used a deadline to finish something, whenever you used a limitation to invent something, whenever you have been able to translate tension into clarity. You have already done all of those things. You do have experiences where stress was useful.

Stress is useful because it changes our focus and our

physiology. It gives us energy and motivation. We notice more and we respond faster. We can work without knowing we are tired or scared. Complication and complexity are reduced, so that annoying voice in your head can stop asking "what if" and instead ask "what now?" Stress responses evolved to keep us safer in the face of danger. They limit our choices in a way that is helpful if we need to do just one thing. Stress responses are a feature, not a bug.

Experience the Benefits of Stress

To understand the benefits of stress, you can take one component of stress at a time and explore a memory when that component was useful to you.

For instance, you could remember a time when you were very alert, a time when your senses were picking up on things you would usually let slide. Take a few moments to write about this time when being alert was a good thing, a thing that helped you stay safe or move forward.

Stress also makes us feel that we have energy, that we can just keep pushing forward. Remember a time when you had all the energy you needed to do what you wanted to do, a time when your energy carried you forward. Take a few moments to write about this time where being energized was a good thing, a thing that helped you stay safe or move forward.

Try one more. Stress can be motivating (that's why we wait until the last minute to do things). Remember a time when you were really motivated to do or accomplish something. Pick a time when you felt the drive to move forward. Take a few moments to write about this time of being motivated, a time when you felt driven to take action.

Stress is not a good long-term strategy

Stress makes it easier to be alert, energized and motivated. These are all good things when you need to take action immediately to manage a threat. They need to be experienced differently over the long term. The same things that make stress effective in the short term can lead to wear and tear on your body, your mental well-being and your social network. It takes a different mindset to run a marathon than a sprint, and it takes willpower and practice to manage your stress in a way that supports you instead of burning you out.

Stress puts limits on your attention. It makes you feel as if the current situation is the only thing that matters. This limited frame makes it easier to pay attention within the stress, but harder to notice what is around it. While focus always sounds like a good thing, if our attention never goes to our peripheral vision, we don't notice the movement that signals either threat or opportunity. Focus also amps up our emotions, and that is only ideal for split-second decisions. More complicated thought requires perspective: we literally need to pull back to see the stress in a wider context before we can access our best reasoning about it.

You are likely to be reading this in a time when there is stress all around you. You are feeling the need to respond to things out of your control. Your brain is working overtime because it cannot predict what comes next. You might feel distracted because you are so busy tracking information about the crisis that you cannot focus on anything else. It takes a process and it takes willpower to push back from your natural responses to work with stress instead of putting up with it.

Thinking beyond the stress

The only reason to manage stress differently is that stress is blocking you from having an experience you would like to have or achieving a goal you would like to achieve. Begin by thinking about something you would do or experience if stress were not a problem. This does not mean pretending that the situation causing the stress has changed. The situation is the situation and you cannot change it directly. What you can change directly is the state in which you approach the situation. So, you will be thinking about what you would be doing in this same situation if stress was not blocking your best thinking or your most effective choices.

The first step in removing stress as a block to the experience you want is to spend a few minutes describing what this situation would be like if you were not experiencing the limits that stress puts on you:

1. How would you feel if you were not feeling stress? Take a moment and think about what would be different in your body if it were not feeling the effects of stress. This might also lead to thinking about emotions, but emotions are harder to predict. It's better to notice that you can remember how your body responds in a state of relaxed energy. Choose a state that you would experience if you were not so stressed. Spend two or three minutes remembering a time you experienced this state (set a timer) and track from the top of your head down through your core to your legs and feet, noticing what is different in this more useful state.

2. What would you be doing if stress were not an issue? Think especially about the planning and outcome formation that often gets pushed aside under stress. You might also notice that there are behaviors that help you innovate or solve problems that you have stopped doing. Again, spend at least two to three minutes walking through your day and asking what you would rather be doing to manage the situation you are in.

3. How would you be connecting with others if stress were not an issue? Stress is affecting your relationships, both personal and professional. People need to become tense to match your stress level, and everyone becomes more

focused on their own point of view. This might be a useful state for a few moments in a crisis (think of a military team), but it does not support innovation or collaboration. And it can be really rough if it becomes a constant state in your home. Take a few minutes (at least two or three) to write about a better quality of connection with people at work and at home.

4. What would you believe about yourself and about the situation if stress were not an issue? Our beliefs govern our expectations which filter our perceptions which determine our choices. Stress limits our perceptions which changes our expectations. The way to recognize this is to think about what you believe now that you have answered the first three questions. How do your beliefs shift when the state in which you approach the challenge changes? Take at least two minutes with this question.

Stress Is Something You Do

When you think of stress as something that happens to you, all you can do is fight it or put up with it. When you think of stress as something you are doing, something produced by your whole complicated self, then you have more choices. You can change the way you do stress so that you optimize it to work for you instead of against you.

You are still reading because some part of this makes sense to you. You know that you have sometimes created stress as a way of motivating yourself or others. You have sometimes used stress about one thing to create a buffer around you that allows you to avoid dealing with something else. You have sometimes experienced stress as significance, a sign that you are engaged in something important.

Once you recognize how stress can serve you, you can make different choices about how to experience it.

You Need a Physical Vocabulary to Describe
a State

If you didn't have some tension in your body, you would be lying on the floor, unable to move. If you experience too much stress, you might find yourself locked into a corner, afraid to move. The trick is to find a level of stress that works for you (not against you).

This exercise scans through your body and your perceptions to build a vocabulary of physical sensations. As you notice different sensations in different parts of your physiology, you become more able to recognize those sensations when they happen again. You can choose to support the state they represent, or to use your vocabulary of physical sensations to make changes. These changes give you access to a different state.

Paradoxically, by focusing on your experience, you also gain perspective on your experience. You are simultaneously highly aware of the details of your experience and yet fully engaged in the experience of observing yourself (and so not caught up in the experience itself). This paradox is the key to mindfulness: when we pay attention to our own experience, we become more able to distinguish between our circumstances and our responses. We also become more relaxed, even when we are paying attention to fear or pain. This is because the observer in us is not attached to the stress we are observing.

There are two ways to coach yourself through this process to explore a time when stress was serving you well. One is to record yourself reading the exercise. If you do this, remember to pause after each instruction to allow yourself time to reflect as you follow the instructions. The other way to do the exercise is to read through it all once, then go back and read one part at a time, writing your responses to each part out either in sentences, or in fragments and doodles.

Think of a time in your life when the amount of stress you were experiencing was a good fit for the activity you wanted to do. You might have been playing in a championship, writing an exam, or leading a team through a challenging project. Whatever you were doing, you had the energy, focus and intensity you needed to be successful.

Remember that time as if it were happening now. See what you see, hear what you hear and feel what you feel as you step all the way back into the particular time and place that were part of this experience. Notice whether you are aware of a picture. Is the picture in front of you or all around you? Are you seeing yourself in the picture or are you seeing the picture through your own eyes? Is the picture moving or still? What colors are you aware of in the picture? Are you aware of light? Where is it coming from? Are you aware of shadows? Notice your focus: is the whole picture in focus or only parts of it?

Now move your attention to your ears. Are you aware of sound as you engage all of your attention in this experience? Is the sound outside you or inside you or both? When you pay attention to outside sound, is it loud or soft? Close or farther away from you? Is it coming from a particular direction? If there are several different sounds, do they fit together (like music) or clash? Is there a rhythm to the sounds? How would you describe the rhythm? The tempo? Are you aware of a voice or other sounds within your head? How would you describe that voice or sound? How does the sound in your head fit into the sounds around you?

Now let's move your attention into your body. We'll start at the top of your head and work down through your body, noticing the physical sensations that are part of this experience. As you start at the top of your head, are you aware of any physical sensations in your head or face? Some people notice tension or relaxation, warmth or coolness, tingling or twitches. You might notice sensation around your eyes or in your jaw. You can let your attention move to the back of your head and move down to the base of your skull and into your neck... (we'll continue all the way down to your toes).

Take one more breath, and scan through the sights, sounds and feelings of this experience, noticing anything else that it would be helpful for you to notice. You might find that this is enough for one session.

If you want more, you can look at the notes you made. For each sensation you recorded, you can ask: could I stay in the same state of useful stress if this were different? Everything you need to support the state is a leverage point. You can make sure it is present when you want that state, and you can deliberately change it when it is time to let go of the stress.

A Different Way to Understand What You Are Feeling

How do you know what you're feeling? Essentially, your body and brain work together to produce changes in your body. Your brain compares the changes to existing patterns and expectations and a word comes into your mind to describe what you are feeling. When a word becomes attached to an experience, it stabilizes your perception of that experience. If you only have a few words that describe emotions, you only have a few groups of experiences that allow you to understand what you are feeling.

You have heard that if you have a hammer, everything looks like a nail. In the same way, if you only have the word "stress" to describe what you are feeling, every tense muscle or tightening of focus feels like stress.

I know you are sure you are stressed. Just look at the situation you're in: of course, you are stressed. But for the sake of understanding how you work, it is worth exploring experiences that are similar to stress in the way they show up in your body or perceptions. If you have many words representing overlapping states, you have more ways to understand what you are feeling. This opens up different interpretations of the situation and what behaviors will have a positive impact on it.

Read each instruction, then take a moment to focus on what changes in your body and senses as you engage with the state you are remembering. Don't just read through and guess what you were feeling: that defeats the purpose. Spend time in the memory of each experience. If you prefer, record the exercise and then let your voice guide you through it.

Experience Overlapping States

Think of a time when you were excited about something. Imagine that time as if it were happening now. See what you see, hear what you hear and feel what you feel. As you build up the memory of where you were and what you were doing, notice the images that come to mind. You might notice whether you are in the picture or looking at yourself, whether the picture is clear or brightly lit or in focus. Notice the sounds that you remember, sounds that might be near or far, loud or soft, sounds that might have rhythm and tone and pitch. Scan down from the top of your head, through your neck, arms, chest, core, legs and feet. Notice areas of muscle tension or relaxation, areas of warmth or coolness, twitches, funny feelings or energy moving in you and through you. Then come all the way back to this time and place. Move your body or say what you are seeing and hearing in this place as a way to come all the way back into the present.

Now think of a time you were aware of being strong and competent. Imagine that time as if it were happening now. See what you see, hear what you hear and feel what you feel. As you build up the memory of where you were and what you were doing, notice the images that come to mind. You might notice whether you are in the picture or looking at yourself, whether the picture is clear or brightly lit or in focus. Notice the sounds that you remember, sounds that might be near or far, loud or soft, sounds that might have rhythm and tone and pitch. Scan down from the top of your head, through your neck, arms, chest, core, legs and feet. Notice areas of muscle tension or relaxation, areas of warmth or coolness, twitches, funny feelings or energy moving in you and through you. Then come all the way back to this time and place. Move your body or say what you are seeing and hearing in this place as a way to come all the way back into the present.

Finally, think of a time you really wanted something. See what you see, hear what you hear and feel what you feel. As you build up the memory of where you were and what you were doing, notice the images that come to mind. You might notice whether you are in the picture or looking at yourself, whether the picture is clear or brightly lit or in focus. Notice the sounds that you remember, sounds that might be near or far, loud or soft, sounds that might have rhythm and tone and pitch. Scan down from the top of your head, through your neck, arms, chest, core, legs and feet. Notice areas of muscle tension or relaxation, areas of warmth or coolness, twitches, funny feelings or energy moving in you and through you. Then come all the way back to this time and place. Move your body or label what you are seeing and hearing in this place as a way to come all the way back into the present.

We often think of stress as different from wanting or excitement or strength. The truth is that these states overlap in our bodies and perceptions. You may have heard about research that shows that people who label their feelings "excitement" make better presentations than people who label their feelings "anxiety." This works because excitement and anxiety overlap in their physiology. When we have more labels for our physical experience, we have more choice about what state we think we are in. We need both the verbal vocabulary (the labels we give to our states) and the physical vocabulary of the signals from our body so that we can choose the most useful meaning for what we are experiencing.

Choose Connection to Tame Your Stress

Stress is addictive. It makes us feel important and energized. It also drains us and puts a strain on our ability to connect with others because we keep pumping energy into the situation instead of generating energy through connection.

Teams that thrive under stress often do not thrive when the stress lessens and cannot continue to strive under continuous stress. Were you ever on a team that won a playoff? Teams that are in the zone together do not experience stress: they experience flow. They train very hard so that under pressure they are aware of the job to be done, not of the stress. Teams that experience stress may win together, but they seldom stay together when the stress is released.

If you haven't put in the conditioning to go into the zone, you can tame stress by seeing it in a bigger context. One way to do this is to intentionally connect to other people. Let your social self be part of how you are motivated and also of how you put your energy to work. The more you are able to focus on the experience of connection to someone you care about, the harder it is to feel the edginess that comes with stress. Stress makes you feel that you are alone under a spotlight, and that everything around you has been blurred out. The balance for that is to intentionally move your attention back into the relationships that have meaning for you. In the next exercise, you'll experience how connection changes stress.

Experience the Power of Great Connections

Record yourself reading this to guide you through this exercise. Or stop reading after each paragraph, close your eyes and allow yourself to fully imagine each part of the experience. To fully imagine means to use your reason and memory to fill in the details so that it seems as if you are physically present in the scene being described.

Imagine that you are standing on a deck, overlooking

a beautiful body of water. The sun is just starting to set, and you can see the light on the water. Down by the water, you see someone who looks and sounds like you. This person is not you, because you are on the deck with me. The person by the water is experiencing a situation that causes them stress.

As you stand here on the deck, you are comfortable and happy. The air is clean and fresh. In the distance you might smell food on the barbecue or hear the sounds of birds. In a moment, you will be visited by three people. Each of these people represents a connection that would be useful to the person you left down by the water, the person who is being hurt or limited by stress. They may be people who are currently part of your life, or people who have been important to you at any time in your life.

As you enjoy the water and the early evening, you see someone you haven't seen for a long time, someone you loved very much when you were a child. This person stops in front of you, smiles, and steps out of their shoes. Step into those shoes, and experience the world through the eyes and ears and heart of this person you love. Look out over the water as you feel the strengths and beliefs of this person move in you and through you, changing your balance and your breath, changing the way you see and hear.

Now you are joined on the deck by someone you love now. This person also smiles at you, and steps out of their shoes. Step into those shoes, and experience the world through the eyes and ears and heart of this person you love. Look out over the water as you feel the strengths and beliefs of this person move in you and through you, changing your balance and your breath, changing the way you see and hear.

Finally, you hear someone approaching and you see someone who inspires you to be your best. This person also smiles at you, and steps out of their shoes. Step into those shoes, and experience the world through the eyes and ears and heart of this person who inspires you. Look out over the water as you feel the strengths and beliefs of this person move in you and through you, changing your balance and your breath, changing the way you see and hear.

As you stand there looking out at the sun on the water, feel the rush of energy and motivation, of meaning and awareness. When you are ready, look at the person down by the water and call to that person. Watch as that person turns at the sound of your voice. Call again, until you see that person moving toward you.

As that person reaches you on the deck, look into their eyes and smile. Reach out and give this person a hug, pulling them all the way back into you so that they are standing in your shoes and you and they are just one person. Notice what changes as you feel yourself settling back into being just one person with all the strengths and resources you have been given. Know that these gifts come to you through intention and relationship and that they are part of you, waiting until you need them to move through stress to achieve satisfying results.

It might take a few minutes to let all the different thoughts and feelings settle after this exercise. When we deliberately form connections between previously unconnected experiences (in this case with the three different people), it can feel like someone has moved the furniture in our internal homes. Take the time you need to get used to how you feel now.

Stress Is a Difficult Gift

The situations that provoke stress in us can be good or bad. We can be offered an opportunity that we really want and feel stressed about how we will live up to it. We can face a time of social upheaval and change, and work desperately to keep ourselves and the people we love safe. We can be faced with terrible decisions to make or devastating health news. We cannot control the situations that cause us stress. That's a large part of what makes them stressful.

The stress that arises in us as a result of those situations is neither good nor bad. It is more like a super power. If you're a geek (like me), you'll know that in every story where a normal human being is given a superpower, there is a period of resistance, a struggle to figure out how to use the power and how to feel about it. Stress is like that. You can love the energy and focus and the feeling of being engaged with something that matters. And you can hate the tension, the sleeplessness, the isolation and the inability to get out of your own head.

Like any budding superhero, you need to practice getting your powers to work for you and not against you. The ability to focus and to drive yourself harder in the short term does not mean you have to cut yourself off from the values and people who are important to you. As you recognize the benefits of stress, instead of fighting yourself, you can bring yourself into a balance that moves between focus and flexibility, between energy and recovery.

Three Things to Remember

1. Stress has significant benefits.
2. You need both an emotional vocabulary and a physical vocabulary to understand stress and how to work with it.
3. You lessen the negative impacts of stress when you put it in the context of your connections to other people.

Chapter 5

Dealing with Other People

You are good in a crisis. You think about the situation. You focus on the problems you need to solve first. You use the best resources available in your brain, body and social self to make choices, take action and support the people around you. But when you connect with those other people, they also connect with you. And the influence they have on you can throw you off your game.

The way we connect with other people is that we synchronize our states so that we can predict each other's behavior and either protect ourselves or collaborate more effectively. This is a feature of the social self that enables both learning from one another and sharing each other's strengths. In earlier chapters, we've explored how other people reflect parts of ourselves that we cannot see and how we can reflect back strengths that they are not sure they have. But that same ability to see things in others that they cannot see in themselves is a double-edged sword. Sometimes it means someone shows you something you did not realize about yourself.

It's disconcerting to have someone else know you better than you know yourself, if only in one small aspect. It undermines your carefully built sense of integration and the power that comes with believing you're one complete person rather than an assortment of different parts. It's important to have a strategy for incorporating what you learn so that you can keep it together, especially when the world around you is not a safe place.

Another way other people can throw us off is that they surprise us with their perspectives. We only have eyes in the front of our head. We'd like to think we can make up for it by turning to see a full 360 degrees. The truth is that we have blind spots (at least one of which is right in front of us) and other people can see things in our situation that we cannot see. They surprise us with information we did not see coming. All surprises interrupt the patterns which keep us grounded and moving.

People also share their states with us, whether or not we want them. This is most true with the people closest to us. With some people, we are naturally guarded. We engage in rapport but it's the rapport of competitors sizing each other up. It doesn't interrupt our self-management because we've built it into the states we hold around them. This is a strategy we cannot use with the people closest to us. When we know people well, we do two things: a) we scan the world for dangers to them in the same way we scan for dangers to us and b) we take on their states so that we can make more detailed predictions about what they are feeling and what it will mean for us.

When someone you love is hurting, you hurt too. When someone you love is celebrating, you scan the situation for any dangers they might be missing while they are happy. They do the same things with you. This is why it is hard to be consistently in any one state when you are with the people closest to you. You tend to balance each other out instead of setting each other up for the risks you might be willing to take individually. This makes it easier to survive but harder to achieve.

Surprise! You Just Lost Your Train of Thought

Remember that your brain works in patterns. The neuroscientists say that what fires together wires together. This means that all the neurons that are active at one time (they fire together) are connected (they wire together). Your brain doesn't just store data: it stores meaningful relationships between data. When you think of your first kiss, you don't just remember the kiss. You remember the situation in which the kiss happened, the sights and sounds and smells. In the same way, experts at any skill build up their storehouse of patterns so that they recognize a meaningful pattern where other people might see random facts. Making meaningful patterns is what our brains do to predict the future so that they can keep us safe and recognize opportunities to meet our goals or live our values. The making of meaningful patterns is so basic that it's what we mean when we say we are thinking: we are looking for relationships that tell us what to expect in a given situation. This is the brain's core function.

What happens when a pattern is recognized and then interrupted? You've had this experience in simple ways. Sometimes you've pulled at a handle while staring at a sign that says "push." Sometimes you've traveled to another country where the traffic comes from the wrong direction or the toilet flushes in a way you've never seen before. There is a moment of confusion between starting to do something the way you always do it and the recognition that you've just done the same thing and gotten a different result.

Did you see what I just did there? You're used to being told that insanity is doing the same thing over and over and expecting a different result. And I have just given you an example that says precisely the opposite: sometimes doing the same thing does get a different result. And usually you're not thrilled about it. You're confused. In that moment, you can't get back to the state you were in and you're not in a new state yet. You are vulnerable.

People don't usually surprise you to make you vulnerable. They are usually not trying to surprise you at all. They are working from within their own patterns and expectations. When those expectations are different from yours, you have a "what the fudge!" moment. You are connected to someone and that connection doesn't feel like a bridge. It feels more like a blast of air from an open window.

It takes a lot of skill and practice to regularly interrupt other people's patterns so that they become open to a change of thought or direction. It's a better use of time to work on recognizing the feeling you get when you've been surprised, and the change in a connection when you have inadvertently surprised someone else. Set a timer for at least five minutes and begin the process by making a list of times you were surprised or confused, and times you surprised or confused someone else. Write about the situation before the surprise, how the surprise happened, and what changed afterwards and don't stop before the timer goes off.

A Change of Perspective

When your own perspective isn't showing you a good way forward, then a change of perspective is a good thing. What about when your perspective was supporting your states and your movement and it suddenly shifts when you connect with someone else? No one feels good when the ground is moving under their feet.

Again, this doesn't normally happen because people are trying to throw you. It takes a lot of cognitive resources to understand someone else so well that you can identify their blind spots and then sneak up in one of them. Most of the time, the people you are interacting with are neither that malicious nor that deliberate. They're not really thinking about you at all. What they are doing is unconsciously processing the difference between their interpretation of your situation and the patterns you are expressing in your communication and state. When they notice a difference, it's like finding Waldo. They feel triumphant and they want to let you know about what they have discovered.

Do you want to know? Imagine you're setting up a project or event. You are grateful that someone sees what you forgot, but being told about it is never fun. You feel surprised and vulnerable and worried about what else might be missing. Of course you're glad that the problem was caught, but you are not happy with yourself for missing something.

We have the same issues with our memories of situations.

In the next exercise, try to capture at least four different perspectives of a family event. Notice where they intersect, and where there are differences. You're probably sure your memory is correct and the others are wrong. That's confirmation bias as it shows up in your beliefs and your body. Our brains look for evidence that matches what we already think. The odds are very good that none of you holds an accurate representation of what really happened. You all hold the meaning that your brain encoded with the circumstances: you remember what your brain prioritizes as useful.

Ask for Alternative Perspectives

Think about a family event or a work event that was meaningful or emotional and that happened in the past six months. Pick something with a positive meaning that is not too deeply personal. You will be likely to find that other people remember it differently, so don't pick the deepest, most important thing.

Begin by writing about the event for at least five minutes, capturing what you remember. Think about where and when it happened, what else was happening in your world at the time, what actually took place, who was involved, and what meaning you drew from it.

When you have stabilized your own recollection by writing it down (it's too late to change your memory now), begin to explore how other people remember it (if they remember it). It's best if you have the chance to ask two other people who were at the event to tell you about it or to write their own descriptions and send them to you. You'll probably find they are curious about the differences, too, and will do it if you promise to show them what you discover.

It's unlikely that there was an objective observer at this event, but you can imagine the perspective of an objective observer. Sit down with the timer set for at least five minutes again. This time, write what you remember as if you were observing it, not engaged in it. Pay special attention to patterns of rapport and influence, to who did what first, and who followed their lead. Describe the different relationships in the situation as if you were evaluating how people would take sides in a meeting.

Now read through your notes about these different descriptions of the same event. How sure are you now that you know what really happened? How sure are you about who had influence and all the different roles played by different people? How sure are you that this event did have meaning?

Finally, scan through your physical sensations now, from the top of your head moving down through your core and into your legs. How do you feel about this experience of seeing the same experience from different perspectives? You might find that you are a little off balance. It takes some time to get used to the difference between what is reliable and what feels true.

How to Keep Your Head

As you have now experienced, people get under your skin and into your head. They don't usually do this to sabotage you. They do this because they are being themselves and noticing things that are outside your awareness. As you become more aware of how other people interrupt your patterns of thought and response, you become more resilient. You can more often notice when you have been drawn into a state or perspective, and make choices about what to keep and what to change.

This will not be enough to allow you to stay the course on the mindset and emotions you want to choose for yourself. A state is the combination of your mindset, emotions, perspective and physiology at a given moment in time. All emotions are states, but not all states are emotional. Stress is a state and so is focus. We use information from outside us to support our states, and our states filter what we notice around us so that we are more likely to hold a useful state. States drive our behaviors.

States are also contagious: we naturally synchronize our

states so that we can understand each other better. This facilitates learning, cooperation and predicting dangers. But it also creates a danger. How do we connect with people who are in states that are not useful to us, states we have worked hard to overcome in ourselves? Panic, anxiety and depression are just some of the states we can catch from the people around us.

If You're Not Leading, You're Vulnerable

The only way to steer your own course is to lead. You can't avoid connecting with others, even though they often hold states that are not useful to you. You need to synchronize states to get value from those connections. But you don't have to synchronize with unhelpful states. You can hold states strongly and repeatedly until you bring others into sync with you.

Here's how that works. We have seen that many states can share similar physiology: excitement, stress, and anxiety, for instance, all show up in our bodies in similar ways. Focus and intensity and anger and fear can also be similar. Physical sensations, balance, breath and rhythm are important building blocks for states and the same blocks can be used to build states that have quite different consequences.

When you connect with people, you will notice changes in your physiology. As you match and mirror what you are observing in them, your physiology will change. If you are aware of these changes, you can then interpret them in a more positive light. Instead of choosing to sync with panic, you can mirror with urgency or determination. Instead of matching anxiety, you can match anticipation or a strong goal focus.

Here's what will happen when you succeed in this kind of matching. People will feel connected and slightly confused. They will notice that something feels different, but won't be sure why. You will have shown up in their blind spot. While they are confused, they are looking for ways to stabilize their experience. You can help by shifting again into a version of the state you are mirroring that has more balance and less tension. Within moments, the connection can settle into the balanced and useful state that you have chosen.

This might seem like too much happening too fast. That's just your mind trying to match the speed at which your brain/body connections work. When you practice, the behavioral patterns happen faster than conscious thought. The trick is to understand that a conversation is less about the words exchanged and more about the states you exchange. And the best way to manage those states is simply to hold two different intentions simultaneously: the intention to connect and the intention to hold states that feel useful for you.

It's not complicated, but it is energy intensive. It means giving up on going with the flow and just feeling whatever you feel. You become accountable to yourself for the way your interactions play out. This can seem like a lot to carry. It is a lot to carry. In a time of crisis you will be surrounded by people who are experiencing strong emotions. Many of them will be focused on venting, not on contributing. Some of them will be struggling to make sense of the situation and some may even be heartbreakingly sad. If you are to hold an intention strongly in the midst of this, expect it to take willpower. Expect it to feel like hard work.

The only thing harder than managing your relationships is letting your relationships disrupt your patterns and pull you out of your intention for yourself.

Three Practices That Lead to More Useful States

These are not insight-based exercises that you do once. These are the kind of exercises you do at the gym: you have to do them regularly to build strength and flexibility in your connections with others. It's a good idea to start with the people that make it easiest for you to practice, and to work your way up to managing your state in difficult emotional situations.

The first practice is intention. This means that before you make a connection, you already know what you want to experience in that connection. The easiest place to practice is with routine work conversations (whether they are in person, by phone or online). Before you make the call or enter the room, it's important that you think through what you want to achieve by having the conversation. I once talked to a manager about his weekly meetings with his direct reports. I asked him what he wanted from the meetings and he said, "The meetings are really for them." I explained that his intention could include supporting his people but that he needed to know what he wanted to be satisfied with his results. As he became clearer about his intentions, both he and his people felt better about the meetings.

As you think about the result you want, you can also think about how you want to get there. What states will be most useful in promoting the result? You'll need a different state to motivate action than you would to get information. Think about how you want to feel and how you want the other person to feel. It may take you a while to think about the possible mindsets, strengths or experiences you want in your conversation. Brainstorm a long list of possibilities, then choose the ones that you feel are most important.

Setting your intention means taking a moment to mentally rehearse what you want to experience in the meeting. Studies have shown that mental rehearsal is very effective in developing skills and priming behaviors. If you are serious about getting a result, you must be serious about detailed mental rehearsal. The best way to get this level of detail is to go into a memory of a time when the states you have identified led to a positive result. As you revisit that time in your memory, play it through as though you were watching a movie. Then step into the movie and play it through again as if you are living it now. Become very conscious of the cues in your body and perceptions that indicate you are in the state you want to be in.

Finally, run through a mental rehearsal of the conversation you want to have. Step into that rehearsal in the way you have just stepped into your memory: see what you will see, hear what you will hear, and feel the physical sensations that will cue you to connect to the state and the outcome that you want.

The second practice is rhythm. It is a paradox that we are seldom conscious of rhythm but we are very sensitive to it. Our brains handle rhythm and timing in ways we do not yet understand. We have different rhythms for voice, movement, breath, blinking and heartbeat. Conversations have rhythms too. You can track the rhythm of a conversation that is not going well, and change the rhythm to change the conversation.

It helps if you begin to notice the rhythm of people's voices. Whether you are watching something on television or talking to family or colleagues, begin by tapping a finger lightly in time to the rhythm of their voices. Just listen as if you are listening to music. Notice when the rhythm shifts, and when it settles. Practice this until it feels natural.

Then practice matching rhythms. Experiment with picking up a rhythm (by tapping with a finger or foot), and then sending it back. You can match rhythms with your voice, or with a gesture, or by deliberately blinking or breathing in the same rhythm. Whatever you do should last only a few seconds. Rhythm creates a strong bond, and you want to practice focusing on the rhythm without getting caught up in the connection.

Finally, practice matching a rhythm and then moving into a different rhythm. Changes in rhythm signal changes in state. It's useful to be able to shift the rhythm so that you can lead into a state that is more useful in getting the result you want.

The third practice is match and pivot. This means taking the same pattern you used with rhythm and doing it with words instead. Begin by practicing repeating a few words or a phrase that another person has just said. Just repeat what they said and then add what you want to say. When you match words, you show attention to the other person. They know you are hearing them. But you also remind yourself: these are not my words and this is not my state. I am connecting to this other person's state.

When you can easily pick up a few words and send them back, you can practice your pivot. To pivot means to keep one foot where you are while you change direction. In conversation, the repetition of a few words grounds the connection and frees you to change the topic or tone. A dramatic change is likely to unbalance the conversation. A pivot is a more subtle shift towards your intention. Repeat, then pivot towards the state or information you want in the conversation. Stabilize that with more repetition, then pivot again to come closer to what you want. Repeat until you have achieved your intention for the conversation.

It Takes Energy to Move against the Flow

All of these practices depend on two things: 1) you have to know what you want and 2) you have to be willing to do the work to get what you want. Some days, this will seem difficult. You will want to rant with the person who is ranting or cry with the person who is crying. Most of the time, you will find that giving up control of your state to "the flow" of the conversation actually takes quite a lot of energy too. You just displace that need for energy from the conversation into your recovery time.

We have all heard some version of the quote that says if you don't know where you are going, it does not matter which road you choose. That's not always good advice except that it points to the truth that when you do know where you are going, you will have to make choices to get you there. Those choices are motivated by two things: your goal or destination and the kind of journey you would like to take you there. Knowing both those things will give you the energy you need to go against the flow.

Three Things to Remember

1. Surprise induces confusion.
2. Different perspectives can throw you out of state.
3. It's better to lead than to defend.

Chapter 6

Your Inner Compass

Who will you be when this crisis is over? On the one hand, the answer to that lies on the other side of a horizon: you can't see there from here. On the other, you know that you are more focused and effective when you work toward goals. The point of reading a book like this is often that you know there is something out there you want to be, and you're not sure how to get there when you can't reasonably expect to see it.

How can you set a specific, measurable, attainable goal when the thing you know for sure is that your situation is going to change? Yes, after a crisis, things get back to normal. But there is absolutely no guarantee that the new normal will be recognizable as the normal we left behind. We are all going boldly into a future we cannot see. Without direction, we are left to go with a flow that is full of danger and uncertainty. The only way to quiet the noise in our brains is to set a direction.

It's time to take stock of what you can use to build a vision of a future that is desirable and realistic. You cannot plan for the big situation to resolve itself in a particular way or at a particular time. You don't know what will work or be useful or even what external resources you can count on to support whatever you decide you want to accomplish. The choice seems to be that you can move forward blindly or be stuck.

Here's a better way to look at it. You can decide who you will be when you reach the horizon. There's a trick here, of course. The horizon is obviously real: you can see it. You use it to keep stable while you walk, and to navigate. But the horizon is not real: it's a perception that shifts as you move. No matter how far away that horizon is, you'll never get there. It's always out in front of you.

And that's why it is useful. It is a constant in a world where everything has changed. There is a line that separates what you can see from what you can't see, and you never get to see past that line any more than you can get to know your unconscious processes. What you can do is use that ultimate point of perception and say, "This is what I am heading toward."

So the "you" that you put out on the horizon is the goal that never shifts, the outcome that makes every step clearer and more balanced because you will never reach it. Before you close this book, before you take the next steps through the crisis, spend a few minutes getting to know the self you want to become.

There are two words people use to describe knowing what you want to be: purpose and presence. At first glance, they seem to be in tension. We think of presence as being open to what is around us and purpose as a way of being active in changing our circumstances. There is a kind of logic in that and well-meaning people often discourage us from wanting something because they are afraid that it will make us value the present moment less. That would be logical if you had limited ability to pay attention to both what you want and what is happening at this moment.

That's not how your brain and mind actually work. You store all kinds of information safely in the background, and you put information to work in the background without thinking about it. The better you know something, the easier it is for it to work in the background. When you know your purpose as well as you know a good friend, then you can trust that purpose to work below the surface of awareness and encourage you to be more present so that you can feed the brain more potential routes to serving that purpose.

Start with a Sense of Direction

What does a compass do? It shows you how to explore the whole of the world, the part you can see and the part beyond your vision. An inner compass will help you think about the whole of your life, the things that you want because life is uncertain and dangerous, and the things you want because sometimes life is really great.

It's not a list of goals. Goals are things we don't have yet and when we focus on them, we often lose sight of everything that we already have and value. The compass is a way to capture all the things you want to be part of your life, including the people, activities and experiences that already exist in your life and add value to it.

You'll find this easier to follow if you take a piece of paper and divide it into four. At the top of the vertical axis, write wellness. At the bottom of that axis, write work. On the far left on the horizontal axis, write relationships and on the far right, write play.

Your compass has true north set to wellness. Without wellness, you don't have the energy you need to form relationships that matter, to create new experiences or to make an impact on the world. It's also true that your inner compass is naturally set to wellness as true north; your brain and body function to keep you safe and alive. We need to set wellness as an intentional goal, because although our bodies and brains are set to seek it, our minds can have competing priorities.

Opposite your true north of wellness is work. We take energy from the world in the form of air and nutrients, and we give it back in the form of work. Think of work as the impact you have on the world, the way you make it safer and create new possibilities. Some of this involves making money (which allows you to be safe and well) and some of it is about making a difference in your family or community.

In the west, between wellness and work, we will place relationship. Our connections to other people interact with both our wellness and our work. Human beings are socially wired creatures and our need to connect what we do with others is driven by being human, not by personality. We feel safer in connection than we do alone (from an evolutionary standpoint we are almost always safer in a group). Our relationships help us achieve wellness and when we collaborate, they also help us make an impact through our work.

The final direction, the east, is play. Play represents our inherent connection to the world we live in. When we play, it is because we are safe and connected enough to risk energy in the service of joy. The benefit of this is that joy can support both wellness and work. It lifts the pressure to perform and moves our focus from surviving to purpose. Our relationships often lead to play (even when we are also working) and play builds relationships.

As you reflect and model the way each of these four directions has shown up in your life, you'll start to build a compass that allows you to form a better sense of who you are and what you want. You will find that you do not live in a two-dimensional world where moving in one direction means sacrificing another. You live as your bigger self, where you can grow in all directions and each direction has a role in enhancing the others.

Draw Your Inner Compass

Wellness. Begin with the top half of your paper. What do you think wellness means? Some people assume that wellness is about being physically fit. They think that a focus on wellness means eating, sleeping and exercising in appropriate ways. Other people assume that wellness means something like "of sound mind and body." They include physical well-being, but they add a requirement for being capable of making good choices about one's life. Still others think of wellness as being fit for the world because you make good moral and ethical choices. They would add a spiritual dimension to well-being.

Now begin to write in words (or doodle images) that represent the ways you want to be well. On the left side of the page, put the things you do with other people that help you be well. On the right side, put the things that bring joy or beauty into your life, the things you do that make you feel connected to life. In the middle, put the practical things you do to maintain your well-being.

Before you move on, take another look and ask yourself: what am I missing? To be well in the world means to have well-being and strength mentally, physically, emotionally and spiritually. If you're not a spiritual person, you may still believe that your ethics are part of how you make the world a safer place. If there's any dimension that you're missing, fill it in before you move to the bottom of the page.

Work. Move to the bottom half of the page. Work represents our impact on the world, our ability to act instead of reacting, to be the cause of what happens in our lives and the lives of other people. Work is related to confidence. When we work, we feel capable and feeling capable feels good. And work is also connected to our sense of legacy, our exploration of the difference that our life could make for others.

Begin to write in words (or doodle images) that represent the ways you want to make a difference in the world. On the left side of the page, put the work you do with and for other people. On the right side, put the things that you create and the problems you solve because you enjoy making a difference with your skills, strengths and ideas.

Before you move on, take another look and ask yourself: what am I missing? To make an impact on the world, you need to have knowledge and information. You need to communicate effectively with lots of different people. You need to maintain some things, and you need to make others that don't exist yet. Take a few moments and think about how you want to achieve more mastery, make an impact, keep things running or develop something new.

Relationships. Focus on the left side of the page. Connecting to others is not a choice we base on personality. It's a choice that's embedded in who we are and how we think as human beings. When we are alone, we often think of other people and imagine their words, thoughts and actions.

Begin to write in words (or doodle images) that represent the ways you want to connect with other people. On the top of the page, put the relationships that support you in being safe and well. These are the relationships that make you feel good about who you are and what you can do. On the bottom of the page, put the functional relationships that help you get things done: the relationships with people at work or in the community that fill in the gaps in your skills or strengths.

Before you move on, take another look and ask yourself: what am I missing? Who else do I want to have in my life or how do I want to add a new dimension to the relationships I have now? How do I want others to think about me now or remember me later?

Play. People who play feel safe enough to give their attention to something that has no immediate practical value. They sometimes experience joy. Joy might only last for a few moments, but those moments shift how we perceive the world and the opportunities available to us. In play we are able to let go of judgment and experience our limits without resenting or pushing against them. Play draws us into the present and makes us glad to be there.

You might have to dig a little for experiences of play and the place it has in your life. On the top half of the page, look for things you would like to do that make you feel good, the things that you enjoy doing. On the bottom half, think about things you love doing even if they are also work. Many people play by solving problems or running an event or creating a better system.

Before you move on, sit quietly for a moment and remember at least one more time when you did something just for the joy of doing it. Add that to your compass.

The Whole of Your Life

Look at what you have completed. It's not a list of things you want: things you don't have but think you should achieve or acquire. It's a dynamic system of things that either make you safer or allow you to enjoy the safety you create for yourself. Everything relates to everything else: building a relationship might add wellness or it might enable a new kind of play or a new achievement at work. Creating something new at work might build relationships with your collaborators or enable you to play in ways that support your health and well-being. You can start anywhere on the compass and trace the impact of something you value as it influences other things you want.

As you look at your compass now, you can see some action items. Whatever the future holds, however circumstances change, there are things you want to do. You are not in control of the situation, but you do have choices about where you will focus, what you will maintain and what you will build with your skills and your energy.

The compass shows you the whole of you: the many different ways you can act to make a difference for yourself and others. It demonstrates that you need all of this to describe the life you want. The next step is to be present in whatever you are doing, knowing that each part of the compass contributes to all of the others.

Choose Role Models for Being Present

What do you think it means to be present? People have many different experiences of heightened sensory awareness. For most, that awareness comes as the inner voice becomes quiet. The world seems to slow down because they are letting more information in. People who are present with us make us feel that all of their attention is with us. People who have presence are people who seem to be living in a more vivid reality than the rest of us. There is no right answer. Presence might make you think of spiritual leaders, or it might make you think of competitors in the zone, or it might make you think of that one person whose charisma changes a room.

Take a few minutes and make a list or mind map of people you think have presence or you think are good at being present. Make notes about what you observe in them and also about how you feel when you are within their influence. This is the first step toward building your sense of who you want to be. You want to be present so that you have access to the best possible information about your circumstances. You want to be present so that you can draw energy from the activities you put on your compass.

Now write at least five sentences that describe you being present. Some of the sentences should describe what other people notice about you when you are present and some should describe your thoughts and feelings when you are present. Don't guess: choose moments in your life when you know you were present and use them to shape who you will be as you are more present in the future.

Connect Presence to Purpose

Now read what you have written about presence. As you do, ask yourself, what do all these people (including me at my most present) have in common? I don't know what your answer will be. But it is likely that what you will notice is that these people who are examples of presence are also examples of what it means to live with purpose.

Purpose is such a tricky word. To say that your life has a purpose either sounds like a fuzzy cliché or it sounds like you have an inflated ego. I understand if you resist the term, but consider this. There are things you do on purpose and things that just happen. The things you do on purpose are the things you are willing to be accountable for, the things you chose to do. We expect more of ourselves when we do things on purpose.

We have said that we can think of our brains as prediction machines that gather huge amounts of data, organize it in patterns, and apply those patterns to predict possible outcomes for our circumstances, relationships and behaviors. Some part of us, deep in our amazing brains, must know the difference between the things we wanted and valued when we got them, and the things we wanted that were not satisfying. What if we thought about purpose as the set of satisfying choices, the set that contains all the things we have wanted that were good things to want and all the things we could decide to want or to do that would satisfy us?

This set is hidden in our unconscious processes. But that does not mean that we can't use it to help us make better choices. We can catch sight of our purpose in the same way we catch glimpses of other parts of our selves. We can notice instincts or feelings; we can see reflections in other people; we can draw connections between our values and beliefs and the choices we make. We can even hear echoes of purpose in our language.

When we say we did something "on purpose," whatever we did had some connection with whatever we mean by "purpose." Our brains do not do random: they work in networks. The word "purpose" is also wired to our use of the phrase "on purpose," even when we don't see the connections consciously.

Experience Being on Purpose
Choose an experience now when you did something "on purpose," when you knew "the right thing" to do and you did the right thing. Trust yourself to choose an experience that will give you an insight or evoke a resource that will be useful to you. As always, you can either write notes on the answers to each question or you can record yourself reading the exercise and then let your own voice guide you through it.

Think of a time you did something on purpose. Notice where you were when you did it and when it was that you did it.

Now look back and notice the behaviors you did when you did that thing on purpose.

Think about the skills, strengths, and resources that allowed you to do those behaviors so that you could do that thing on purpose.

Think about someone you like and respect. How would they describe this thing you did?

Imagine a blogger or newspaper wrote a piece on this thing you did on purpose. What would it highlight?

Think about the beliefs you hold about yourself and the world that support those strengths, skills and behaviors so that you could do that thing on purpose.

Consider your identity. Think: "I am a person who..." and finish the sentence with a reference to this thing you did on purpose.

Finally, take a deep breath and allow an image, sound or feeling to come into your awareness as a symbol of this experience of being aligned with your purpose. Take a few moments and notice what is different in you when you are on purpose. Use the symbol you picked to bring back all of the experience so that you stay on purpose.

Use Your Sense of Purpose to Make Good Choices

Our brains are realists: they make predictions based on what has already happened. Our minds can be optimists. We need to believe the future can be better than the present if we are to make it better. The person you are when you are on purpose is a deliberate optimist. And that is the person you need to see on the horizon, the person who calls you to keep making choices to make things better.

Good goals prime our brains to look for opportunities, not just dangers, and they cause us to reach for new strengths and abilities in order to meet them. Particularly in a time of uncertainty, we need to know what we want in order to know who we are and what we are capable of. We need to set goals that define the quality of our experience as much as the quality of our results.

Your sense of purpose can help you choose stretch goals, goals that motivate you not just to achieve, but to grow so that you can achieve. These stretch goals have to be specific enough that you will be able to recognize them as you achieve them and general enough so that they don't depend on what you will find on the other side of the crisis horizon. You can't know what you can't know, so you need to ground your forward motion in things that you will be able to choose in whatever situation you end up facing.

Think for a moment of the symbol for your experience of being on purpose. Hold it clearly in your thoughts. Become wide awake and present. And now look at your inner compass and ask: what do I need to do next? You can write for at least five minutes to capture your response, or you can make a list of at least three things that are stretch goals based on your purpose and compass. One path can be blocked. Two paths are an ultimatum: do this or do that. But three paths show life that you mean business: you're going to keep moving toward your purpose even when some of the roads you planned are blocked.

Three Things to Remember

1. Set goals in the context of the whole life you want.
2. Presence makes you more aware and more connected.
3. Purpose drives both motivation and satisfaction.

Chapter 7

What Comes Next?

We started with the idea of the horizon; the limit to our vision of the future. In a crisis, much of the future is hidden from us. We don't know what will come next.

I hope you're finishing with a different sense of that horizon, as a direction that calls upon you to keep moving, as the end of a story that has yet to be told. You don't know what will come on the other side of the horizon. You do know now what kind of person you will be, what kind of choices you will value, and what goals you will pursue on this side.

A great goal requires that you get stronger: that you build skills and perspectives and flexibility as you move toward the goal. Whatever goals you have chosen, I hope they make your journey more satisfying. The road ahead will have twists and bumps and maybe some dead ends. You will need more strength than you have now to travel it.

That's okay. You haven't reached that part of the story yet. By the time you get there, presence will have extended your perceptions and purpose will have made you stronger. You already know the answer to one important question: How will I grow stronger today so I am ready for tomorrow?

There's one more important question. What will you build with the day in front of you? It's not just a goal; it's a way of owning what you can do and making something a little better. If a pandemic teaches us anything, it is that small connections can cascade to make a disproportionate impact. This is true of small improvements. One small step leads to another, and the world gets better. And so will you.

Recommended Reading

Ariely, Daniel. (2010) *Predictably Irrational: The Hidden Forces That Shape Our Decisions.* Harper Perennial.

Barrett, Lisa Feldman. (2017) *How Emotions Are Made: The Secret Life of the Brain.* Houghton Mifflin Harcourt.

Berg, Insoo Kim and Peter Szabo. (2005) *Brief Coaching for Lasting Solutions.* W. W Norton.

Burton, Robert A. (2013) *A skeptic's guide to the mind: what neuroscience can and cannot tell us about ourselves.* St. Martin's.

Damasio, Antonio. (2005) *Descartes' Error: Emotion, Reason, and the Human Brain.* Penguin Books Reprint.

Doidge, Norman. (2007) *The Brain That Changes Itself: Stories of Personal Triumph from the Frontiers of Brain Science.* New York: Viking.

Gilbert, Daniel. (2006) *Stumbling on Happiness,* New York: A. A. Knopf.

Gladwell, Malcolm. (2005). *Blink: The Power of Thinking without Thinking.* New York: Little, Brown and Co.

Johnson, Steven. (2004) *Mind Wide Open: Your Brain and the Neuroscience of Everyday Life.* New York: Scribner.

Kahneman, Daniel. (2011) *Thinking, Fast and Slow.* New York :Farrar, Straus and Giroux.

Lieberman, Matthew D. (2013) *Social: Why Our Brains Are Wired to Connect.* New York: Crown.

McGonigal, Kelly. (2015) *The Upside of Stress: Why Stress Is Good for You, and How to Get Good at It.* New York: Avery.

Rubinstein, Dan. (2015) *Born to Walk: The Transformative Power of a Pedestrian Act.* Toronto, ECW Press.

Shaw, Julia. (2016) *The Memory Illusion: Why You Might Not Be Who You Think You Are.* London: Random House.

About the Author

Linda Ferguson is a coach, a trainer, a storyteller, an author and a community builder. She combines exceptional expertise in metaphor, narrative and rhetoric with a broad knowledge of current thinking in NLP-related fields, including positive psychology, solution focused coaching, personality typing, and behavioral economics. Ferguson mixes best practices from these fields to enable clients to think and achieve differently. For almost twenty years, she has been building an extraordinary community of diverse people who are committed to knowing themselves better so that they can make a difference in the lives and work of other people.

A graduate of Trent University (B.A.), the University of Western Ontario (M.A.) and the University of Toronto (Ph.D.), Ferguson has been teaching communication for more than thirty years. Her dissertation on W. B. Yeats (1990) was called *We Sing Amid Our Uncertainty*. It has been excellent preparation for a career helping people think and communicate in ways that keep them resilient and purposeful.

Previous Title

Living Your Purpose: The Heart of NLP

Living Your Purpose walks readers through the five principles
at the heart of NLP. Neurolinguistic programming (NLP) is
the study of how people make change on purpose. In applying
NLP to your own life, you simply assume you have what you
need and the problem is to find it. Whether you are in pain,
confused, stuck or in pursuit of a goal that seems impossible,
there is only one problem. You have not yet made a conscious
connection between that situation and the resources that will
lead to a satisfying outcome.

This is a book for everyone who has ever wished that NLP
could be clear and practical and rooted in evidence that what it
teaches really works.

ISBN: 978-1-4602-1456-5

Would You Like to Connect Again?

I am so glad that you made it this far with me. Thank you for reading this book. If you found it helpful, please spread the word to the people you know who want to get better even in a crisis. It would be wonderful if you left a brief review at Goodreads or on the site where you purchased it.

If you would like to stay connected, you can find me on the Internet. I'm active on social media and post regularly to my blog and podcast. I even send out a weekly newsletter with one short article and links to new resources and #freeNLP Zoom training. You can find everything at www.nlpcanada.com.

I'm also happy to connect on social media:

@nlpcanada on Instagram

@nlpcanada on Twitter

https://www.facebook.com/Nlpcanada

Or email me at linda@nlpcanada.com

TRANSFORMATION

The *Resilience* Series

The Resilience Series is a collaborative effort by the authors of Changemakers Books in response to the 2020 coronavirus epidemic. Each concise volume offers expert advice and practical exercises for mastering specific skills and abilities. Our intention is that by strengthening your resilience, you can better survive and even thrive in a time of crisis.

Resilience: Adapt and Plan for the New Abnormal of the COVID-19 Coronavirus Pandemic
by Gleb Tsipursky

COVID-19 has demonstrated clearly that businesses, nonprofits, individuals, and governments are terrible at dealing effectively with large-scale disasters that take the form of slow-moving trainwrecks. Using cutting-edge research in cognitive neuroscience and behavioral economics on dangerous judgment errors (cognitive biases), this book first explains why we respond so poorly to slow-moving, high-impact, and long-term crises. Next, the book shares research-based strategies for how organizations and individuals can adapt effectively to the new abnormal of the COVID-19 pandemic and similar disasters. Finally, it shows how to develop an effective strategic plan and make the best major decisions in the context of the uncertainty and ambiguity brought about by COVID-19 and other slow-moving large-scale catastrophes. The author, a cognitive neuroscientist and behavioral economist and CEO of the consulting, coaching, and training firm Disaster Avoidance Experts, combines research-based strategies with real-life stories from his business and nonprofit clients as they adapt to the pandemic.

Resilience: Aging with Vision, Hope and Courage in a Time of Crisis
by John C. Robinson

This book is for those over 65 wrestling with fear, despair, insecurity, and loneliness in these frightening times. A blend of psychology, self-help, and spirituality, it's meant for all who hunger for facts, respect, compassion, and meaningful resources to light their path ahead. The 74-year old author's goal is to move readers from fear and paralysis to growth and engagement: "Acknowledging the inspiring resilience and wisdom of our hard-won maturity, I invite you on a personal journey of transformation and renewal into a new consciousness and a new world."

Resilience: Connecting with Nature in a Time of Crisis
by Melanie Choukas-Bradley

Nature is one of the best medicines for difficult times. An intimate awareness of the natural world, even within the city, can calm anxieties and help create healthy perspectives. This book will inspire and guide you as you deal with the current crisis, or any personal or worldly distress. The author is a naturalist and certified forest therapy guide who leads nature and forest bathing walks for many organizations in Washington, DC and the American West. Learn from her the Japanese art of "forest bathing": how to tune in to the beauty and wonder around you with all your senses, even if your current sphere is a tree outside the window or a wild backyard. Discover how you can become a backyard naturalist, learning about the trees, wildflowers, birds and animals near your home. Nature immersion during stressful times can bring comfort and joy as well as opportunities for personal growth, expanded vision and transformation.

Resilience: Going Within in a Time of Crisis
by P.T. Mistlberger

During a time of crisis, we are presented with something of a fork in the road; we either look within and examine ourselves, or engage in distractions and go back to sleep. This book is intended to be a companion for men and women dedicated to their inner journey. Written by the author of seven books and founder of several personal growth communities and esoteric schools, each chapter offers different paths for exploring your spiritual frontier: advanced meditation techniques, shadow work, conscious relating, dream work, solo retreats, and more. In traversing these challenging times, let this book be your guide.

Resilience: Grow Stronger in a Time of Crisis
by Linda Ferguson

Many of us have wondered how we would respond in the midst of a crisis. You hope that difficult times could bring out the best in you. Some become stronger, more resilient and more innovative under pressure. You hope that you will too. But you are afraid that crisis may bring out your anxiety, your fears and your weakest communication. No one knows when the crisis will pass and things will get better. That's out of your hands. But *you* can get better. All it takes is an understanding of how human beings function at their best, the willpower to make small changes in perception and behavior, and a vision of a future that is better than today. In the pages of this book, you will learn to create the conditions that allow your best self to show up and make a difference – for you and for others.

Resilience: Handling Anxiety in a Time of Crisis
by George Hofmann

It's a challenging time for people who experience anxiety, and even people who usually don't experience it are finding their moods are getting the better of them. Anxiety hits hard and its symptoms are unmistakable, but sometimes in the rush and confusion of uncertainty we miss those symptoms until it's too late. When things seem to be coming undone, it's still possible to recognize the onset of anxiety and act to prevent the worst of it. The simple steps taught in this book can help you overcome the turmoil.

Resilience: The Life-Saving Skill of Story
by Michelle Auerbach

Storytelling covers every skill we need in a crisis. We need to share information about how to be safe, about how to live together, about what to do and not do. We need to talk about what is going on in ways that keep us from freaking out. We need to change our behavior as a human race to save each other and ourselves. We need to imagine a possible future different from the present and work on how to get there. And we need to do it all without falling apart. This book will help people in any field and any walk of life to become better storytellers and immediately unleash the power to teach, learn, change, soothe, and create community to activate ourselves and the people around us.

Resilience: Navigating Loss in a Time of Crisis
by Jules De Vitto

This book explores the many forms of loss that can happen in times of crisis. These losses can range from loss of business, financial security, routine, structure to the deeper losses of meaning, purpose or identity. The author draws on her background in transpersonal psychology, integrating spiritual insights and mindfulness practices to take the reader on a journey in which to help them navigate the stages of uncertainty that follow loss. The book provides several practical activities, guided visualization and meditations to cultivate greater resilience, courage and strength and also explores the potential to find greater meaning and purpose through times of crisis.

Resilience: Virtually Speaking
Communicating When you can't Meet Face to Face
by Teresa Erickson and Tim Ward

To adapt to a world where you can't meet face to face – with air travel and conferences cancelled, teams working from home – leaders, experts, managers and professionals all need to master the skills of virtual communication. Written by the authors of *The Master Communicator's Handbook*, this book tells you how to create impact with your on-screen presence, use powerful language to motivate listening, and design compelling visuals. You will also learn techniques to prevent your audience from losing attention, to keep them engaged from start to finish, and to create a lasting impact.

Resilience: Virtual Teams
Holding the Centre when you can't Meet Face-to-Face
by Carlos Valdes-Dapena

In the face of the COVID-19 virus organizations large and small are shuttering offices and factories, requiring as much work as possible be done from people's homes. The book draws on the insights of the author's earlier book, *Lessons from Mars*, providing a set of the powerful tools and exercises developed within the

Mars Corporation to create high performance teams. These tools have been adapted for teams suddenly forced to work apart, in many cases for the first time. These simple secrets and tested techniques have been used by thousands of teams who know that creating a foundation of team identity and shared meaning makes them resilient, even in a time of crisis.